MW01195144

Getty and Townend Masterworks

The Songs of Keith Getty, Kristyn Getty and Stuart Townend

Arranged by James Koerts

The collaborative efforts of Keith and Kristyn Getty, along with Stuart Townend, have produced long-lasting modern hymns for the church. The combination of deep, biblical texts and memorable melodies has enabled these songs to become a significant part of the musical vocabulary of many churches. They gently reach down and touch one's heart with the truths they so boldly proclaim. The lyrics to "The Power of the Cross" exemplify this:

> This, the pow'r of the cross:
> Christ became sin for us;
> Took the blame, bore the wrath.
> We stand forgiven at the cross.

The truths of the cross are simple, yet profound. The cross is where justice and mercy meet. The forgiveness that Christ freely offers to all was purchased at such a great price on that cross. It is through Christ's suffering that one becomes free.

> What a love! What a cost!
> We stand forgiven at the cross.

James Koerts

Produced by
Alfred Music
P.O. Box 10003
Van Nuys, CA 91410-0003
alfred.com

ISBN-10: 0-7390-8353-8
ISBN-13: 978-0-7390-8353-6

Cover Photo
Wine grape: © stock.xchng.com / OeilDeNuit

(Approx. Performance Time – 2:30)

ACROSS THE LANDS

(YOU'RE THE WORD OF GOD)

Words and Music by
Stuart Townend and Keith Getty
Arr. James Koerts

(Approx. Performance Time – 2:45)

BY FAITH

Words and Music by
Keith Getty, Kristyn Getty and Stuart Townend
Arr. James Koerts

(Approx. Performance Time – 2:30)

COMPASSION HYMN

Words and Music by
Keith Getty, Kristyn Getty and Stuart Townend
Arr. James Koerts

(Approx. Performance Time – 2:45)

COME, PEOPLE OF THE RISEN KING

Words and Music by
Keith Getty, Kristyn Getty and Stuart Townend
Arr. James Koerts

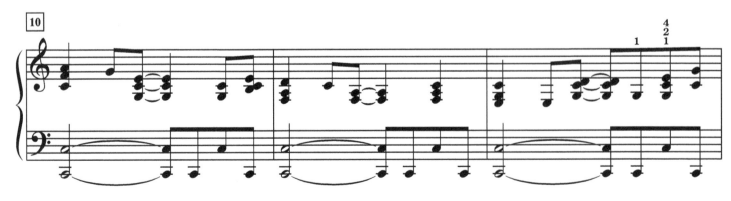

(Approx. Performance Time – 3:15)

How Deep the Father's Love for Us

Words and Music by Stuart Townend
Arr. James Koerts

(Approx. Performance Time – 3:00)

In Christ Alone
(My Hope Is Found)

Words and Music by
Stuart Townend and Keith Getty
Arr. James Koerts

Tenderly, with conviction (♩ = 72)

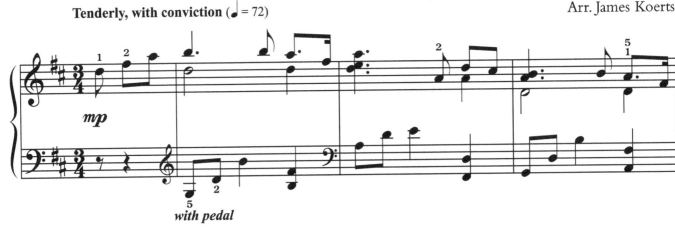

(Approx. Performance Time – 2:15)

My Heart Is Filled with Thankfulness

Words and Music by
Keith Getty and Stuart Townend
Arr. James Koerts

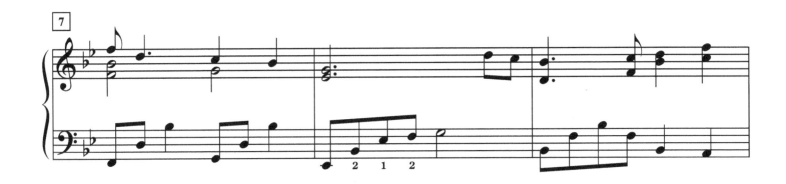

(Approx. Performance Time – 2:30)

O Church, Arise

Words and Music by
Keith Getty and Stuart Townend
Arr. James Koerts

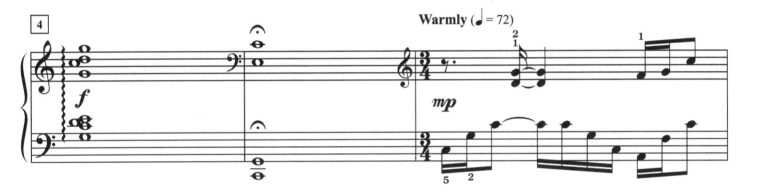

* "Onward, Christian Soldiers," by Arthur Sullivan

(Approx. Performance Time – 2:30)

The Power of the Cross
(Oh, to See the Dawn)

Words and Music by
Keith Getty and Stuart Townend
Arr. James Koerts

(Approx. Performance Time – 3:45)

SPEAK, O LORD

Words and Music by
Keith Getty and Stuart Townend
Arr. James Koerts

(Approx. Performance Time – 3:45)

Still, My Soul, Be Still
with
Be Still, My Soul

Words and Music by
Keith Getty, Kristyn Getty and Stuart Townend
Arr. James Koerts

* "Be Still, My Soul," by Jean Sibelius

(Approx. Performance Time – 2:45)

See, What a Morning
(Resurrection Hymn)

Words and Music by
Keith Getty and Stuart Townend
Arr. James Koerts